ESSAY ON RIME

BOOKS BY KARL SHAPIRO:

PERSON, PLACE AND THING

V-LETTER AND OTHER POEMS

ESSAY ON RIME

ESSAY ON

RIME

BY KARL SHAPIRO

REYNAL & HITCHCOCK, NEW YORK

Parts of this essay have appeared in Partisan

Review, The Kenyon Review, The Sewanee

Review, and Poetry: A Magazine of Verse.

PRINTED IN THE U.S.A. BY CORNWALL PRESS, CORNWALL, N.Y. I

TO MY WIFE

CONTENTS

This is a tract on the treble confusion   1
In modern rime. The premise that our verse
Is in decline has not, I am convinced,
Been honestly attacked or well defended.
Critics in particular have minced matters
By acquiring all the authority to talk.
I ask you not to balk at my presumption
But with a certain reasonable kindness
Toward the subject to attempt this study.
I think it is high time that everybody   10
With a true love of rime assert his views.

In the mid-century of our art we leave
The park behind and rest beside the zoo
Of rarities. Very fortunate for us
That monsters of their own peculiarities
Perish. Yet they remain. As visitors
It is our privilege to stare at the adept
Keepers and the odd assortment of the kept.

Some chimeras are real, some counterfeit.
White unicorns are drinking from the brook;   20
Bellowing from its cage the anthropophagus
Rushes at us. These creatures, certainly,
Deserve the status of actualities. But look,
What is that perpendicular snake, that woman
With hot eyes gleaming in her viscera?
The question is one of language. No conception
Too far removed from literal position
Can keep its body. Ideas are no more words
Than phoenixes are birds. The metaphysician
Deals with ideas as words, the poet with things,   30
For in the poet's mind the phoenix sings.

Now whether the egg of modern criticism
Precedes the squawking chicken of semantics
Is a scholar's quiz, but insofar as Meaning
Has tried to adopt Poetics, the plot thickens.
But can the science of definition relate to
Poetry, even obliquely? To science belongs
The isolation of knowledge, to art belongs
The isolation of beauty; nor is it likely
40 That even in this aviary can we mate two
Creatures of such opposite feather. The owl
Has many thoughts, the woodlark only songs.

Perhaps Lucretius felt that through the means
Of language highly charged, more could be said
Of his philosophy than prose could prove;
His form is rare but not considered specious.
Horace and Pope, this pair may be adduced
As poets who argued in the voice of rime
And argued well. But poets prefer to roost
50 In arbors rather than the tree of knowledge.
That bard expelled from Socrates' Republic
Is held sweet to the world; for understand
That dialectic is the foe of poetry.

If, then, I am accused of paradox
In forcing argument to the cast of rime,
My only answer is that criticism
Has charted poetry into dangerous narrows
And dashed its own brains out upon the rocks
Of absolute meaning; that this essay is given
60 In protest to the semantic muse, a pharos
Perhaps to dialectics but to poetry
A siren of the Homeric cut. To use
Language emotionally and not as number
Is my intention: my hope is to infuse
Criticism with pleasure, sense with clarity.

One verse of Shakespeare's is a matter for
A Vatican of wonder and research.
I cannot take the scholar's perch or view
The present field like critics, ex cathedra.
My aim is to suggest, not to pronounce   70
Sentence, or trounce the brothers of my trade;
My wish is but to call a rose a rose
And not a trope; my only rationale
To answer homemade questions and not those
Put by poetics old and new. I trust
I have not bit off more than I can chew.

This essay deals with three major confusions:
In Prosody, in Language, and in Belief,
Each part discussing five aspects of rime
As follows. Under Prosody: the first,   80
Its English application; second, three
Important studies; its forms and chaos third;
Its metric fourth; and fifth and last its cults.
Next under Language: first its idiom,
General and personal; second, personality
And style; its grammar third; rhetoric fourth;
And fifth, translations and false dialects.
Finally, under confusion in Belief
These headings: first, the failure in belief;
Second, the new and substitute beliefs;   90
Personal systems third; our dialectic
And criticism fourth; and fifth and last,
The dead hand and exhaustion of our rime.

THE CONFUSION
IN PROSODY 1

1. APPLICATION OF PROSODY IN ENGLISH

By prosody I mean behavior, rime's
Deportment, movement, melody. Those poets
Of classic times whose verses always scanned
Were by the nature of their speech restricted
To admirable scansions. Greek demands
The measurement of sounds; Latin's assortment
Of dance-like rhythms is a Latin law.   **100**
We know that from the mansions of antiquity
Much has been looted, and not all of marble.
The very nomenclature of their prosody,   ANCIENT
Unsuited as it is to ours, we claim,   PROSODY
And garble modern textbooks with misnomers
That once applied with accuracy to Homer's.

Riming of sounds was not sought by the ancients
Whose speech abounds with echoes in the suffix;
Excess of melody they had without
End-echoes and these tonic innovations   **110**
Which to our more discordant tongue adds music.

The measure of English verse can take two forms
And only two; the first by count of eye,   SCANSION BY
The other by count of ear. By count of eye   COUNT OF EYE
We read the written units of the line
And stress the printed accent where it falls.
The treasure of English verse far and away
Fits in this first design and is the norm
And standard metric from the time of Chaucer
Down. In the second form, by count of ear,   **120**
We hear and do not visualize the stress.
Sung poetry dearly loves this freedom, ballad,
And children's chant, and every rapturous air   SCANSION BY
That rose from Shakespeare's heart. When poetry   COUNT OF EAR
    shares

Its passion with pure music, it does not pause
To hold its breath by pentametric laws.

How then among the great themselves, this first
Confusion in the art of rime? The chorus
Of Milton's *Samson,* endlessly discussed,
130 Flows by the count of ear and no more scans
(But parse it if you can) than Hebrew. Wordsworth
Under the spell of prosody maintains,

And Coleridge likewise in the *Christabel,*
A rediscovery of the rime of folk,
Yet neither Whitman, Blake nor Burns invokes
Arithmetic. Attempt the Browning metric,
Hippity-hop for eye and ear at once,
A sweet and difficult tongue; or Hopkins' tour
De force, sprung rhythm—count of ear of course.

140 Nor is it accurate to charge the great
With misconstruing metric; by and large,
Whether they write for eye or ear or both,
True poets are loath to probe their own designs
And to commit autopsy on their lines.
Yet for our understanding of their skills
Little enough of value has been left
To guide us. I take it as a fact of weight
That in five hundred years of noble rime
Not one large work of prosody appears
150 Or is considered requisite to the art!
Rime scholarship was born in the mid-part
Of the nineteenth century, less than a hundred years
Ago. Of many studies in this school
Let us consider three: Bridges', Lanier's,
And Saintsbury's; on Milton, rime, and prose.

For mastery of method Milton stands
Supreme in English. He is the scholar's poet.
No metric more exactly planned exists
Than his. A perfect mechanism turns
Paradise Lost, his solar masterpiece,   160
Written in blindness and by count of eye.
In Bridges' study of the poem we learn
What feats the decasyllable performs,
What variations in the pace and why   BRIDGES
The music of this epic is particular   ON MILTON
To its own law and will not satisfy
The *Comus,* for example. Shakespeare's line,
Far from precise is more auricular
And contradicts the strict Miltonic scale.

Keats knew that Milton took more liberties   170
With diction than a lesser Englishman
Would dare, and thought the *Paradise* a curio,
Albeit mighty. Likewise, we may call
The framework of the poem a fiction wrought
Too intricately for common use. Perfection
Is the abuse of form, but for my part
I think the discipline of Milton's art
The purest guide to rime. Bridges discovers
The innumerable permutations of the line
And indicates how by a shift of weight   180
Cliffs and enormous fragments of the verse
Are hurled headlong, or brought to rest, or stopped;
The speed of falling angels, the travail
Of Satan laboring upward through Chaos,
The sweet slow step of Eve in Paradise
Milton designs by stress and shift of stress
And always to the count of ten. Again,

9

To study metric in the *Paradise*
Is one precise approach to count of eye.

190 Metric by count of ear is best described
By musical notation. In Lanier's
LANIER'S *Science of English Verse* the solecisms
SCIENCE OF Standard in texts of prosody are replaced
ENGLISH VERSE By notes and rests, minims and crotchets, signs,
Quarters and eighths of sound. This poet observed
That words of song rather obey the song
Than syllable: thus units short and long
Change quantity to suit the sounded measure,
And poems themselves are marked with signature
200 And definite time, in which occur the stop,
The slur, the inverted turn, appoggiatura,
Symbols of purer melody than rime.

It is the reader's interest to determine
Which poems will scan by notes and rests and which
By syllable. The macron, or long mark,
And breve, or short, used in accentuation
Are suitable for count of eye. *The Rape of
The Lock* conforms exactly to this scheme
But, for example, *The Forsaken Merman*
210 Does not. The shape of poetry may be proper
Or negligee, but lyric verse per se
Pursues the wild *La Belle Dame Sans Merci.*

The author of *The Science* penetrates
Still further, recommending that the length
A POSSIBLE Of line and stanza are capricious forms
NEW METRIC And somewhat arbitrary; even for us
This is quite revolutionary to doctrine,
But more so is his prophecy that rime
Will mate with prose and probably create
220 A yet-undreamed-of measure for our verse.

Time has already shown the strength of this
Prediction, for in the prosody of prose
Mines of new rhythm lie, as Saintsbury shows.

This beloved scholar was, I think, the first
To assay methodically the beat and pattern
Of English prose—nor am I qualified
To judge the value and the wealth of effort
Contained in this important book. A vast
And even dangerous masonry confronts
Him; all the history of written speech,
Cathedrals of it. What obtains for us
Is Saintsbury's hope that we may verify
The curve of prose, and thus reduce the line
To elements and measurable parts. Each block
Of brickwork must be broken to the ground,
Examined and reset. In prose the form,
As in the architecture of a church,
Is lost; the noble thing itself remains.
Rime has a cruder principle: the poet
Composing ascertains the very plan
And in the fibre of the thing he writes,
Enfolds it. Myriad as are the forms of verse,
The cadences of prose are infinite.

For better or for worse the poet no longer
Holds it unorthodox to break the mold.
The worn designs of stanza, all the rubbed
And exquisite tracery of another hour,
Though they will never pass, already yield
To different metal; and the shivering shocks
Of change, plying the crowbar with good will,
Indicate something of the new power which
Saintsbury wrote of and Lanier foresaw.

SAINTSBURY
ON ENGLISH
PROSE
RHYTHMS

230

240

250

Grammars of rime, describing the inflection
Of English speech, sometimes refer to "rising
Rhythm," a phrase convenient as a clef.
Analyzing the term it comes to mean
Not pitch or quantity but both. The ways
In which a single word or words are sounded
Depend on syntax or position; thus
260   Though usage sets pronunciation, pitch
May modify or flatten the accent.
The tendency of English is to strengthen
The volume of the accent and to stretch
Its tone. So tractable is modern diction

RISING   That quantity is no guide; it may be shown
RHYTHM   That in America there is no one school
Of modulation. Emphasis is the rule
If any. When rising rhythm was the norm
(From Middle English down) it took the flow
270   Of light stress followed by the heavier stress.
Today the inclination is to force

DECLINE   Both accents to the limit; long loud beats
OF RISING   Repeat like tomtoms, and indeed the urge
RHYTHM   Is toward the primitive. The muscle-tone
Of prose controls the muscle-tone of rime,
And speech being at tensile strain, the wires
Of verse are tuned up to a tight staccato.

Poets differ rightly on the extreme adoption
Of a new rationale. Change is the test
280   That tries the skill of masters; but we have proof
In Eliot, for example, that the triumph
Of a new form is certain. Poetasters
Flinch at his brilliant prosody, being conscious
That rising rhythm is slightly less than optional
In the twentieth century. Nevertheless a few

Of the best craftsmen take the older view,
While others argue for its full disproof.

The early Imagists, with the gauche behavior
Of saints and radicals, were no gentle crew;
The tapestry of rising rhythm they tore   290
To shreds, and little of the loom they left,
Much less the weft of the traditional
Scansion. Constraint was not the principle,
And long before their manifesto laid
The law down, certain purely transitional
Phases set up as separate guilds, at least
Several of which had serious influence
And prestige which has not as yet decreased.
Before touching on these let us examine,
If possible, the ecology of their form.   300

Form is the build of any organism,
Living or dead, of a whole tree or a leaf,
A whole poem or a word. In prosody,   IMAGIST
Where all is motion, form is the interaction   PROSODY
Of all the parts of rhythm that produce
The sensory effect of single rhythm. In past
Eras of art the chief preoccupation
Was not with craft, not with mechanics, but
With the end-product, its effect and use.
Some time in our grandfathers' generation   310
Rime took to looking at itself as form,
X-rayed its own anatomy, discussed
The trend of art toward science, until by dint
Of hypnotism a means became an end.

Resultantly, all that once had seemed inherent   BREAKDOWN
And lawful in composition now appeared   OF METRIC
Not stale but actually incoherent. Form
Became the atoms that bombard the senses;

The composer became a compositor; the line
320 Crumbled to bits of syllable, and design
All but supplanted count of eye and ear;
Until the day arrived when many a poet
Sat with a lapful of pied type and lead
And puzzled over the fragments, while some few
Descanted on the attraction of the new.

4. METRIC

Thus part of the new metric wrecked its forms
And part, often with most consummate grace
Proved its intentions.—Here let us return
To those who earlier inferred a case
330 For prose metric in rime, and seek the clue
If any between their prosody and ours.

EARLY Donne's rhythms he bequeathed three centuries
INDICATIONS Ago, and yet they lay untouched until
OF A The present time; all literature between
NEW FORM Completely shuns his versification. Why
And how does it seem applicable to ours?
The answer, I believe, is accident.
His nature forced his genius to invent
A prosody of thunderclaps and bullets
340 Which is now recognizable; and perhaps
The current interest in Donne relates in part
To this one characteristic of his art.

DONNE Yet scholarship has shown that count of eye
Is actually his method, and that the mark
Of his robustness is the deliberate twist
Of rising rhythm. Thus, stresses in the line
Collect like stones to block an easier flow.
That Donne ran counter to the prosody
Of his own age, I think must be dismissed.

14

The Browning question is yet unposed; either   350
Like Donne, he undertook to modify
The prevailing metric (and in this case to fuse
The count of eye and ear) or else he glozed
Over his prosody; or even really used   BROWNING
The third alternative, the prose. His metric
Is more than the unique, and I submit
That study of *The Ring and the Book* may throw
Light on the latter method. Possibly Pound
Owes more to the Victorian than is found
At first glance in the *Mauberley* and the *Cantos*.   360

Hopkins' influence, on the other hand,
Is actually small, in metric as in belief.
Except for such devices as his end-rime,
Which hints at the phonology of Greek,   HOPKINS
His impress is not great. The dissonant vowels
Have caught us, but is it not fortuitous
That Hopkins and not Emily Dickinson
Is credited with this invention? The chief
Value of Hopkins' prosody to our rime
Lies in a prophecy. He foresaw a break   370
In rising rhythm, and stamped the count of ear
With unmistakable boldness on our minds.

Likewise Walt Whitman, wearied of the fake   WHITMAN
And effeminate forms of Europe and New England,
Suddenly burst forth in that declarative metric
Which shocked polite society. A comparative
Study of Bible English and *Leaves of Grass*
Does not, however, reveal kinship, as some
Maintain. His prosody in the main may be
Clocked by the metronome, though curiously   380
His later rhythm approached the count of eye
Scansion. Bridges detected, for that matter,

A similar trend in Hopkins' later poems;
But neither seriously poached on this preserve.

Whitman's metric is maladroit, at times
As flaccid as the gentle curve of Longfellow's
Evangeline, but at its best the strongest
Link in American prosody. In fact,
If any one poet fathered a new form
390   And freed us from the traditional, it is he;
But neither Whitman nor his close descendants
Have set a practicable norm; in lesser poets
Than the Good Gray the open rhythm works
Hardships upon the rime, and in our day
Reflects but poorly on the prototype.

By far the two great prosodists of our age
Are Joyce and Eliot, both of whom are bound
In filial respect to Ezra Pound.
A proper treatment of the metric media
400   Of these three would necessitate a work
The size of an encyclopedia. Here

EMERGENCE
OF A
NEW FORM
Let us attempt a precis of the forms
Of the first two, bearing in mind that both
Approach from opposite sides the same objectives.

Eliot began with count of eye, but early
(We hear of his destroying couplets) turned

ELIOT
To more immediate music. One corrective
He introduced, the even step of French,
Opened a window on the Parisian schools
410   Which at the same time looked upon the English
For an exchange of form; an old artesian
Spring began to flow between these tongues,
Replenishing both. Yet this was incidental
To the main tide of metric. Poets abroad
Were all establishing prose cadences

In rime, some we have seen with ruinous
Effect and Eliot and a skillful few
With revolutionary success. The clean
Conversational voice of the American
Once and for all outlawed the late-Victorian   420
Lilt. Tennyson, Swinburne and the like
Went down, their age discredited by all
Who scorned the sweet Arthurian melancholy
Of smooth roundel and plaster elegy.

When it appears, the study of the music
Of *Ash-Wednesday* should compel the minds of all
Poets; for in a hundred years no poem
Has sung itself so exquisitely well.
The frightened beauty of *The Hound of Heaven*
Is not the sister of this psalm that sings   430
In the ascendant voice of sad desire; but hear
How every step enjoins the heart to follow
Whether it will or not, or start or stop
Or turn again or kneel and genuflect.
And who will parse the broken measure of
The Waste Land, our world-weary masterpiece
In which the very metric tells the tale?
Who will devise the necessary scale
To read this rime as Milton's has been read?

If this is done, some clue may be provided   440
For even more structural and inwoven verse.
It was Virginia Woolf who said (and meant
It well) that the *Ulysses* was a great
And magnificent failure. Wilson, for another,
Hints at the same decision, and yet he shows
That the full data needed for such a view
Are not amassed. This intricate and vast
Design to many seems the white elephant
Of prose; to me it seems a thing of rime

450 Entirely. Much of my argument depends
On this; that Joyce establishes a new
Rhythmical idiom, and qualifies or ends
One chapter of prosody. In the second part
Of this essay I hope to demonstrate
That even more than this, he evokes a speech
Which is perhaps the poetry that Lanier
Thought he could hear far off, and tried to teach.

Ulysses is a polyhedron, a thousand
Faces, and some of these the scholars', and one
460 The prosodist's. No single work in English
Debates and illustrates so many forms
Of prose and rime, or so concerns itself
With craft and method, running the lexicon
Of metric. It is a textbook and a guide,
Yet it remains to find within the whole
Whether there lies concealed a rhythmic type
Or only a dictionary of movement. Assuming
That Joyce has *not* evolved the sought-for norm,
Yet for his virtuosity alone
470 And for the ponderous impact of his art
On much that follows, and for his piety
Of scholarship, the licenses of mood
He fought for, we must honor him, a force
As great as any in rime's present course.

The wide and liberating influence of
Ulysses and the studies it provoked
Must in the end account for just as much
Good prosody and bad as Eliot's rime.
Note that direct descendants of this pair
480 Are few; their touch will linger in the deft
New poets, however. Auden, for one, employs

AUDEN   Braces of proselike forms to shape the older
Measure to his own uses and designs.

18

I recommend the metric of *The Malverns,*
A soliloquy of firm and pliant lines
In which both short and distant observation
Are practicable; here birds can fly and bones
Mutter, and armies of the dead recant
With equal voice; nor could these words and stanzas
Precede Eliot and Joyce. Conversely, much   490
That fails in modern rime is traceable to
Their names, such as word-games and word-charades.

And there are those beyond the pale of change
Who grew, like Yeats, outside the planetarium   YEATS
Of newness. He loved and kept a certain range;
He sang by ear as simply as the great
By tortuous system and did not care for numbers.
He and James Joyce were twin antipodal stars
Who swam in a single heaven, scarcely aware
Of one another. Each slumbers and both shine   500
But Yeats without the display of satellites.
Yet in his age, we know, he gave his hand
To the young Englishmen whose contours owed
Nothing to his effulgence; and so slept.

5. CULTS

It argues poorly for the lesser lights
That all their brilliance could not concentrate
In one full ray, or do no more than splash
The broken lengths of color into our faces.
Though some have strength that penetrates and
     burns,
The total is aberration. Visual art   510
In them subsumes the entire act of rime.
As one at the optician's stares through lenses
And sees a dozen depths of the same chart,

These peering poets no longer trust their senses

VISUAL Except through trick refraction or pure focus,
PROSODY Depending on their malady. But not
To err by ridicule, let us cite cases.

Preoccupation with the looks of words
Is a naive and primitive delight.
520 Before the age of presses and type-faces,
When Romans wrote from left to right or both,
Words were sometimes as much designs as names.
Monks in their gold illuminations spelled
Fables in single letters; nor was it held
Absurd by poets three hundred years ago
To shape a poem into a crucifix,
An altar or a pair of wings. To show
The inherent self-consciousness of modern style
In this connection, look at the extreme
530 Of Cubism first and Cummings its exponent.

This poet is most concerned with the component
Integers of the word, the curve of "e",
Rhythm of "m", astonishment of "o"
And their arranged derangement. In Rimbaud
The vowels appear as colors on occasion,
In Sitwell motions. A school of prosody
Threatens to dwell on hidden properties
In dipthongs, semi-colons and italics.
One may or may not challenge this esthetic,
540 But Cummings is no frivolous poet, no fool
At rime. A studious and ascetic mind,
He works at his obsession brilliantly,
CUMMINGS Continues to delight, amuse and anger
The anthologist and advanced practitioner,
And even the humorless critic can afford
To say that Cummings has his own reward.
But morally considered, is it not a danger

20

To atomize the language, construe its forms
As ions, and in the process to beget
Brain-poems of such a nature? Let us look twice   550
Before we adulate the alphabet.

Consider also *The Testament of Beauty*,
A wise and lovely poem too much unread
By us; for Bridges was a craftsman's poet   BRIDGES
And went with modern metric. But note however
The word obsession in the prosody
Which in the end involves his masterwork
With private spelling. What we see in this
Is that the laureate hypnotized by both
The sweet accent of obsolescent rime   560
And the fad of visual prosody of our time
Mixed past and present in an original tongue
Which touches the eccentric. But for the rest
This even dissertation is sung in verse
New and mellifluous, a credit to the best
In Georgian versification and our own.

The central cult of visual rime is that   OBJECTIVISM
Self-styled Objectivist, the purest medium
Yet to emerge from the chaos of forms.
This, as I fathom it, makes that use of words   570
Which Cubism makes of letters. The tedium
Of typography again is broken down
Into design, a rationale that betters
Description in the painter's sense, at least.
Words become things, apples and shoes and **rain**,
An asterisk becomes an electric light!
In this world vision reigns, nothing is right
Except the visible. The object is the thing,
The means of understanding is eyesight.

Lawrence in part partakes of this technique,   580

21

Using it to best advantage in such poems

LAWRENCE As *Tortoises, Wedlock, Snake, Bavarian Gentians,*
Perhaps the most beautiful and enduring of
The Imagist-Objectivist anthology.
The school was doomed to failure but it fashioned
An instrument of style with which the best
Illuminated their monkish manuscripts.

But for a full course in objectivism
We go to Carlos Williams, a professor
590 Of focal points and solids. Many a lesser
But far more popular poet has failed to find
The angle of his terrible microscope,
WILLIAM And (if this is not irrelevant) I for one
CARLOS Have stared long hours at his discoveries
WILLIAMS That seem at times the germs of serious science,
At times the baubles of the kaleidoscope.
A red wheelbarrow, a stone, a purple plum,
Things of a fixed world, metaphysics strange
As camera perception, in which no change
600 Occurs in any image. And prosody yields
To visible invariables; motion fails,
And metric, a fallacy in a static mold
Freezes itself to dazzling shapes, grows cold.

From voyeurism in rime it is one step
SELF- To self-concern, self-imitation. The finest
IMITATION Are quite susceptible. Spender, for example,
Doubles his tracks in all the poetry
Subsequent to his earliest. Marianne Moore,
An objectivist at heart, is seen to pore
610 Over her splendid jewels of rime. Eliot
Himself in the *Quartets* (in my opinion
His most depressing prosody) makes shift
Of rhythms one thought he had exhausted ten
Or fifteen years before. Symptoms of doubt

Lie in reiteration; we sense confusion,
The anxiety of the sensitive to mistakes.
Rather a false step in the right direction
Than circumspect retreat, procrastination.

For prosody as for any form of art
The test is patent: the verse must justify   620
Its use. The verse must equal the whole poem.
It cannot fall below itself or, worse,
Exceed itself. The fashion is to think of   THE TEST
Metric and rime as if no separation   OF PROSODY
Exists in the one process of creation.
That is a critical fiction. At every pause
The poet rechecks the current of the line
As much for metric as for melody,
As much for melody as for sense. The laws
Of any phase of rime are general first,   630
Conditional to the language of its era,
And personal second. To accuse our poets
Of failure in either aspect is unfair
And inaccurate. The magazines are fecund
With serious invention and intention.
The fault, if we must lay the blame, lies more
In the extant violent changes of our speech.
For those who can no longer "shore these fragments,"
Search and discovery are the rule. Our share
Of master prosodists is so far fair,   640
Of mediocrities enough. But teaching
Cannot control the course of rime or reason;
Its function is to try to, and in season
Help keep the house of art and clear the air.
I venture this hypothesis; that rhythm   THE DIRECTION
Flows but in one direction, and that from prose   OF RHYTHM
To rime. The opposite is upstream, against   IN LANGUAGE
The grain of language and the course of change.
The measure of prosody is the current speech,

650 The cadences inherent in the voice
Of one particular generation. Each
Has its own standard, and no choice exists
Between the past and present. Before he sang,
Man spoke, and wrote his deeds before his songs.
The fountain of rime wells from a central source,
The language of understanding; all else proceeds
From this, from the time of David to our day,
And whether in epic, psalm, or roundelay.

THE CONFUSION IN LANGUAGE 2

In one of the most widely circulated
Anthologies of current rime, a speech,   660
The actual peroration of a man
Fated to die, is set within the text
Beside the most exemplary and abstruse
Of modern poems. Vanzetti's broken English
Seen in the context of self-conscious art
In company with the works of gifted minds
At perfect ease, argues a new confusion.
By what philosophy the editor
Attempts to hold this tragic martyred thing
A hostage to the literary cause   670
Is, in a sense, our present argument.
For much of modern rime denotes this bent
To cancel out the distance and the line
Between the language of spontaneous nature
And that of formal artifice. So basic
A solecism cries out for explanation.

Compare the plea for innocence in a play,   SPEECH
Bassanio's for instance with the words   AND POETRY
Vanzetti used before the New England court.
One lives and dies in the imagination;   680
Its reference to existence is oblique
And only by suggestion can impinge
Upon the behavior of the audience.
The other is what the audience knows as *real*,
A fact of the statistical world, as like
An actor's agonizing as true blood
To a splash of crimson paint upon a dress.
Our editor pursues the rule of thumb
Allowed by poets themselves in his collection.
Some can no longer verify the news   690
Except by dramatization; they report

Events as symbols of events, and speech
As poetry. Lacking the prime restraint
Of artists who process experience
Before using it raw, they yield to haste,
Lay out the poem with scissors and with paste
Like so much copy for the linotype.

The question is one of language. In the past
Prose had a separate rhetoric, rime had caste;
700   The stage was not the agora and vice versa.
Not even the rustic at the play would think
A tragedy history, and though an embittered ode
Might cost the author's head, it was a thing
That held to its linguistic mode. Satire
Was not the pistol of straight accusation,
And hate itself was filtered through the skin
Of grammar. So much the worse for us
Whose poets converge on every medium
Of linguistic expression and swarm across
710   The Rubicon from art to actuality,
Not stinting to bear off the documents

ART AND
ACTUALITY Of the new trivium, Sociology,
Psychoanalysis and Economics. To quote
Is an accepted practice of our rime,
As if poetry needs the authority
Of laboratories and the latest news
Of battle and the rights of the majority.

I speak of those innumerable epics, large
And small, which crowd into the latest row
720   Of poetry books upon the wall; of wild
Auricular prophecies of the idea-mad,
The humorless hymns to government in particular,

POETRY AND
INFORMATION The bread-and-butter verses of the poor
In talent; of those who speak in deference
To dialectics, to whom a billboard ad

Has multiple reference, and who find in Alice
An allegory and not an innocent child.

Suspect the novelist the title of whose book
Is lifted from a sermon or a play:
His backbone bends in an apology.   730
Suspect the poet who wallows in symbology
And reinforces what he has to say
With "indigestible portions"; who takes phrases,
Sentences, paragraphs and passages
Into the soft gray matter of his brain
And over them secretes his nacreous pearl.
The prominent symbol of our verse is "bone."
How few successes lead our failures on.

The broad use of the raw untreated data
Of science and of whole experience   740
Expresses a more serious confusion
In rime than the chaos of prosody.
To redefine the general idiom
And separate it from the personal
In poetry seems imperative in our day.
We cannot justify our own excesses
By citing connoisseurs of bric-a-brac;
What they have rescued from the drift and wrack
Of all the past or the immediate present
Is their own property; nor does their need   750
Imply ours necessarily. Even to those
Who thought they saw, like Whitman, the Just City
We owe no public debt. His oratory
On democratic vistas and geography
Is as particular to his character
As vocatives and the wind-blown beard. The pity
Of *Leaves of Grass* is that the straw is eaten
And the good wheat left over by our poets.

The wide style of the dry Americana,
760　Appealing as it is to messengers
Of the official muse, really encloses
A special doctrine of philosophy

As scholarly as Emerson's. But who
Except Hart Crane has tasted the pure manna
Of *Song of Myself,* the naked seed of rime?
When Whitman had the nation on his brain
He served us ill, in my opinion; his leap
Into the personal infinite, however,
Saved him from drowning in his Susquehanna.

770　There is a general idiom to all rime,
A special idiom to one generation,
And, thirdly, the idiom of the single pen.
The poet who does not know by sure instinct

The first, is headed for the rocks of prose.
How many a gallant prelude or frail lyric
Is overturned for ignorance of the sea
Of language. The poet who neither feels nor knows
The flow and current of the second kind
Falls to mere manners and nostalgia.
780　But he who cannot use the first and second
To personal advantage shows no mind
For poetry as the function of one heart.
If anonymity is indeed a failing,
And so we think today, the greater part
Of our anthology is left unsigned;
Its poems appear as nameless synonyms
In the faint collective effort of our art.

I do not here attempt the definition
Of rime, which is the province of esthetics,
790　But to point out its ratio to language.
In the mathematical sense, rime is a power,
Prose raised to the numerical exponent

Of three or six or even n, depending
Upon the propensity of the literature
At a particular time and on the bent
Of the particular poet. It is therefore
A heightening and a measure of intensity.
In the physical sense, rime is the nuclear
And vital element of speech and prose,
The very protoplasm of the tongue,
Or that organic substance which survives
The structures it creates. Words are as lives,
Deaths and mutations, and the poet learns
Through search for life, the biology of rime.
In the theological sense, rime is the ghost
And prose the flesh of language. Poets may boast
That they have known the mystic rose of good,
The blessed face of truth, the host of beauty;
They press the oil and elevate the wine,
For poetry like philosophy is divine
And wells up from the uncreated will.

But these approximate metaphors signify
Little: our argument is to divide
That which is general to the idiom
From that which is specific. In the science
Of textual criticism research is made
To solve disputed authorships and sift
The personal from the common style. The aid
Of generations of grammarians
Is here invaluable; for their trained eye
Almost can mark the verse where Shakespeare
    stopped
And Fletcher took the pen. Collaboration
Was not unusual in that age of rime;
The stage demanded bombast, violence,
Blood and loud laughter simultaneously
With puns, linguistic humor, tenderness

Margin notes:

THE RATIO
OF RIME TO
LANGUAGE

800

810

TEXTUAL
CRITICISM

820

And fluted phrases of protesting love.
The tapestry is whole, but in defiance
Of their collective workmanship we find
830 Here the Marlovian touch and there the scrawl
Of Kyd, or Jonson's cipher, and over all
The unblotted letters *W.S.* Each name
Holds itself high above that century
Of mad soliloquy and brocaded death.
The great survive the idiom of their time.

BALLAD   Only the literature of a gifted folk
Is really nameless; ballad or gay refrain
Or those heart-heavy fruits of tragedy
Of olden times, the genius of the Scotch;
840 Hymns of the earliest English and the monks;
These are the anonyms of rime. To seek
The signature of such an art is aimless;
It is itself the idiom of their time.
Folksong is fieldsong and the stuff of fairies,
And Barbara Allens are not Highland Marys.

2. PERSONALITY AND STYLE

But poets are name-proud craftsmen; Greeks and
  Jews,
Chinese and Arabs time out of mind have penned
The symbols of their authorship against
Oblivion. One significant conceit
850 Of Tudor rime was that its pages were
Imperishable, and we choose to think our own
At least as durable. In the complete
Edition of the poetry of one man
We are confronted with a life, for style
Is ever the clue to personality,
A certain combination to the safe

Of private character. And if indeed
Calligraphy provides a kind of key
To individuality and conduct,
What then does whole creative poetry?   860

Style was originally the implement
Of writing, the actual tool of penmanship
Held in the hand. Our usage of the term
Thus symbolizes that with which the word   STYLE
Is written. In a limited modern sense
Style may be called the repetition of
Characteristic habits; speaking more broadly,
The very impress of the character
Upon the work in progress. There arises
In every mind a tendency of difference,   870
The germ of the unique; our small erratic
Twitches of diction or more happy graces
Lead from the fictive norm to actual cases.

Seek in the symptoms of excessive style
Morbidity; in the English of Carlyle
Hysteria, and in Emerson's tortured prose
The manic drive of absolute belief.
What witch pinched Robert Browning, and what
    grief
Beat at the golden doors of Hopkins' heart?
Truly these things are set in style, and clearly   880
Rime can preserve and recapitulate
The acts of poets; for language at such pitch
Unmasks the character and lays bare the face
Which legend, out of goodness, often hides.

In modern art what is phenomenal   MULTIPLE
Is not the loss of style but its increase   PERSONALITY
And wild diversity. Or can it be
That the question is one of personality?

Certain it is that in a single mind
890   We do not look for multiple expression,
At least without uneasiness. To find
Deliberate inconsistency, swift changes
Of heart, facile adoption of new forms,
Is, on the surface, reason to call in
The analyst. An album of Picasso
Shocks by variety; and if such a master
And influence in the arts of paint and words
Can so transmute his media, what remains
For any mere practitioner but to follow
900   Suit? For the disciples of the multiple
In style mistake the growing pains of skill
For versatility. Auden at times alludes
To this confusion in the character
Of modern man: it is indeed a cause
For serious study of our esthetic laws.

Auden, a man of many aptitudes
And that convincing artistry which draws
A following, himself has set us models
So variform as to deny identity
910   To style. The immediate influence of his name
Is probably as great as any single
Force in contemporary rime. Like Joyce
MULTIPLEHe lectures from the lexicon of forms
STYLEAnd illustrates his books with elegiacs,
Ballads and jingles, tragedies and odes.
This is concern with method and the quest
For the lost Eurydice of character;
Genius indeed is an inconstant spirit
But seldom in all the course of rime has man'
920   Altered his very language to conform
With every mold or idea of the poem.
Style is the man: it is erroneous
And false to nature to play false with style.

If one had never heard Polonius,
Vicious Iago, foul-mouthed Falstaff
Or noble Antony speak out, and if
For the first time he gazed upon their words,
How could he fail to recognize the name
That gave them life? As late as the Edwardian
In English verse the use of single style   930
Was taken for granted, but one more generation
Saw the decomposition and analysis
Of meaning, personality, and form
In art. No guardian of the ages past
Could stem the universal change of heart
Which led us toward our schizophrenic end.

3. GRAMMAR

The question is one of language; the breakdown
Of speech into the parts of speech, and writing
Into the ordered structures which we use
Is, in the calendar of time, a late   940
Development. It is supposed that lines
And sentences preceded words. Inscriptions
And ancient manuscripts compress and fuse
Together the separate integers of meaning
We know as words; and by increase of science
Self-conscious grammar comes to rule; the leaning
Toward the more formal and more regular
Becomes apparent; usage is firmly fixed
And literature as the last authority
In right or wrong asserts itself. But grammar   950
Like prosody is a methodical afterthought,
A winter flower of language. Just as no book
Of metric guided the Elizabethan
Poet, so was there nothing of a code
Of grammar to correct or caution him

Except those made by false analogy
On Greek and Latin. Rime in the vulgar tongue
Is richer and more fruitful to the art
Than purest orthodoxy. Chaucer wrote
960 In what then seemed an uncourtly dialect;
To us indeed his triple negative
Is still a barbarism. To recite
The foremost poets is frequently to speak
In slips and solecisms, albeit the flawless
Chatterton or the decorous Gray abstain
From the locutions of the street. But who
Would call the grammar of Othello lawless?
The living speech fashions its principles
On circumstance and pure necessity.
970 Neither the weak conventionality
Of proper schools, nor the Johnsonian
Dictatorship of English, nor the argot
Of journalism, the latest Volapuk,

GRAMMAR   Practical Basic or such lingua franca
AND   Can in reality separately affect
LICENSE   The eventual grammar of the poet's book;
But all of these and more become the melt
Of rime. Each writer is, in this respect,
An arbiter of the tongue; not a free hand,
980 Not an authority, but, by grace of ear,
One who lends emphasis to forms. And if
By chance a new construction in a verse
Takes root elsewhere, it is fortuitous,
A lucky flower sown by a good hand.
Not grammar, right or wrong, rescues the verse
But verse the grammar.

                    In every age of rime
Poets have employed constructions of their own,
Useless to prose, inversion being the chief
Of these. Not till the present century

Was it thought necessary to avoid   990
Such an expedient and to conform
Wholly to the syntax of conversation.
In part we lay our reaction at the door
Of the Victorian and Edwardian tribe
Whose influence penetrated to the last
Georgian. Inversion suddenly saw itself
A Dorian Gray, a monster in disguise.
One can indeed condone the indignation
Of the early moderns; when we consider Dowson
Twisting his grief into a villanelle,   1000
We feel embarrassment. "Fruits and flowers among"
To our more literal ear seems better left
Unsaid. Yet is it just as well that rime
Rejects the entire principle of inversion?   INVERSION
I think not, for in poetry half the magic
Lies in the balance of the phrase. When Auden
Writes "Call us not tragic" he reclaims
A form not only dear to art but new.
Correctness dulls, precision often maims
The poem; nor can the grammar rule the rime;   1010
It is the poem that sets the grammar right.

4. RHETORIC

Yet grammar is but the stem of rhetoric
And rhetoric the leafage of the tree
Of language. I do not use the term in any
Pejorative sense. The beauty of an image,
The functioning of a simile, paradox,
Abstraction, epithet, vocabulary,
Punctuation itself, these are the parts,
But hundreds more, of rhetoric. The interaction
Of myriad forms, like dancing leaves and flowers,   1020
Creates the full expression called the poem.

37

Rhythm belongs to rhetoric; it is forbidden

In prose, for instance, to prepare the cadence
Or to exact the prosody as in rime;
Similarly in prose the tropes are hidden
From the eye. But poetry obtrudes these forms
In full upon the senses and with full care.
The mind recoils from the poetical
In every art but poetry. Emerson's
1030   Essays commit this gross indecency
Time and again; the reader blindly gropes
Through drapes of darkened rhetoric and comes
Exhausted to the outside. The euphuist,
The stylist and the gongorist defeat
Perfection by their pedantry, in the end
Smothering themselves to death in their own tombs.

Here we return to Joyce, the modern Lyly
To some, to others the mighty sphinx of words.
To him we put the question: Do you proceed
1040   From rime to prose or prose to rime or both?
The riddle I believe is just; whoever
Sees in *Ulysses* willy-nilly form

Has not coped with the book as composition.
The poet takes every measurement of a word,
Weight, sound and size, before setting it in
Its preordained position in the line.
The novelist works in larger scale; the mass
To him is greater than the particle;
Nor does he dare, for fear of interrupting
1050   The narrative momentum, to attract
The eye upon a snag of rhetoric.
Joyce measures every inch; each line can pass,
By virtue of its word-by-word impact,
As poetry of the highest skill. (I speak
Of all the chapters of the book in which
He does not parody deliberately

The prose of others.) Emerson is a freak
Of English rhetoric in that what he sought
Was prose incrusted with the craft of rime;
But Joyce begins with rime, proceeds with rime   1060
And ends, as I believe, with rime. If one
Is forced to stop upon a word because
The eye or ear is caught there; if a phrase
Creates a visible image in the mind;
If by a fractional motion of a form
The heart is stirred; or if the sense of beauty
Dilates in pleasure at the artifice;
And if by repetition, emphasis,
And open predomination of device
These forms are made overt and multiplied,   1070
Then what one reads belongs by aim and method
To rime. Nor does this indicate the worth
Of the particular poem. Many a lame
And halt example of inferior verse
Is well-conceived as rime but ill-begot.
In such a case we say the man has failed
His mark. We are concerned here with *intention,*
And I assert that Joyce wrote as a poet
Whether he made the grade or not. Invention
Floods his books; he honors Ezra Pound;   1080
The name Ulysses symbolizes poetry;
Dedalus is the poet par excellence
Of his own world. In short, all that is found
In these disputed pages well equates
With much of poetic method that we know.

If possible it is best to predetermine
Whether the writer names his work a poem
Or something else. It is a fad to show
Parts of the Bible versified and hacked
To lines of even length. Nothing could be   1090
More typical of the new vulgarity,

Or clearer as a symptom of confusion
In language than this error. There is no fact
To demonstrate that any such intention
Existed in the minds of the translators
Who gave us God in English. By some crude
Analogy to the diction of Shakespeare
Some critics and anthologists presume
That poetry was the norm of speech for scholars
1100 As well as playwrights. Hence our attitude
That Paul and Jeremiah can be construed
With Milton and Sandburg as "literature."
When ordinary men reverse their collars
They are not priests; neither can prose and rime
Interchange natures by a shift of dress.
The breakdown is severe, and indirectly
Joyce is as much to blame as any man;
The price he paid for greatness is too dear;
He has his separate triumph, but for the rest
1110 His name is followed by an ugly crew
Of verbal terrorists and learned fools.
Should one review *Ulysses* with cold eyes
He would discern a discipline as strict
As any in modern art. To our own shame
We have divided him among the schools
And left the book unlearned. It yet remains
For one to justify his masterwork
And carry forward what he gave to rime.

In passing, let us mention Eliot
1120 Whose influence on our rhetoric is as small
As his impact on our belief is great.
I cannot guess the cause, unless it is
That English as he uses it in rime
Is personal in the highest and best sense.
One would be rash to imitate a style
Which signs its name at every even pause.

The man whose impress on our rhetoric
Has for a decade dominated verse
In London, Sydney and New York is Auden.
One cannot estimate the consequences   1130
Both good and bad of his success. To open
A current magazine of rime is but
To turn to Auden; and this is not a fad
But some kind of distemper in the practice   VOCABULARY
Of modern poetry. Let us examine one   IN AUDEN
Salutary effect, vocabulary,
And one pernicious influence of his style,
Abstraction.—English wording in the years
Preceding his arrival wore the mask
Of the pre-war nostalgia, a survival   1140
Of the effete in verse, unless it bore
The plainer scent of pure Chicago sweat.
The glance in England was behind; abroad,
Before. Few thought of now as pertinent
To the immediate speech, until a set
Of more or less Oxford radicals unloaded
Their gear of games and books and politics,
Blazers and alcohol and hockey-sticks
Into the lap of middle age. The effect
We know; but when the confusion was decoded   1150
Auden stood out the clearest of the young
Spokesmen. For the first time the radio,
The car, the sofa and the new highway
Came into focus in a poem as things,
Not symbols of the things. The scenery changed
To absolute present and the curtain rose
On the actual place, not Crane's demonic city
Nor Eliot's weird unreal metropolis,
But that pedestrian London with which prose
Alone had previously dealt. Thereafter   1160
Vocabulary took on a modern lease
And opened doors to rooms in which there sat

Such highly contemporary and intelligible
Poets of the age as Barker and MacNeice.

RHETORICAL
ABSTRACTION
IN AUDEN

On the other hand, consider the results
Of Auden's reintroduction of abstraction
Into our rhetoric. From the particular,
The substantive and the difficult commonplace
He moved upon the general and from thence
1170 To an almost Spenserian and occult
Prosopopoeia. Yet in himself this form
Was purposeful for the most part; in the case
Of those who followed it was not. A poet
Who uses the attributive adjective
To signify a concept plays with terms
Rife with philosophy, and beclouds his art
With shades of dialectic. Auden at first
Used the abstraction as a metaphor,
Concretely and with humor, but the figure,
1180 Full of the serum of old melancholy,
Distended in its shell and burst. Thereafter
The capital letter moved across his lines
As ponderously as German nouns; adverbs
Took on the bold appearance of real things,
And pronouns masqueraded as ideas.
The personal development of an English poet
Became almost immediately the folly
Of all who wrote in verse. It needed but
The authority of his name to break the lid
1190 And let the malignant vapors from the box.
Consider for instance the innocuous word,
A common noun in this case, *history;*

THE WORD
"HISTORY"

Though Auden keeps it such, by subtle change
It gradually acquires the vast range
Of signification of a word like *God.*
Auden has written poems on *hell* and *law*
But these thus far are innocent of corrupt

Generalization; but *history* has achieved
A currency in our rhetoric the like
Of which I think must be unparalleled   1200
In rime. I won a wager once that opening
A magazine of verse at random, one
Could put his finger on this word, and used
Moreover in some sense of mystery
Which would defy interpretation. Surely
An all-purpose abstraction is a form
Dear to the tired mind that must malinger
And precious to the talentless; how can
The imitator well resist the coin
Left over by the rich in art? Abused,   1210
Misused and uglified a thousandfold,
This counter passes for the purest gold
From poem to poem, until by reputation
It has acquired the superstitious force
Of the highbrow password. *History* is but one
Of Auden's ill-starred words. *Luck* is another.
It should be mentioned finally that the chief
Rhetorical influences of this poet inhere
In such forms as the paradox, the surprise
Adjective, and the contradiction in terms.   1220
Successful usage justifies these structures
In Auden only, but it is my belief
That fundamentally they express a lack
In rhetoric; for the tyrannical epithet   TYRANNY OF
Relies upon the adjective to produce   THE EPITHET
The image; and no serious construction
In rime can build upon the modifier.
However matched and well-met are the words
In such a phrase, the end-product is loose.
The high thin rare continuous worship of   1230
The self-absorbed is an example which
Outside of Auden has become the craze.
The tigerish blazer and the dove-like shoe

Is obviously the prototype for those
Who speak diffusedly of *the childish night,*
Meaningless children, the albino crow,
The riding flesh, and *the unmurdered rose.*

5. TRANSLATIONS AND FALSE DIALECTS

Historians of our literature will, I hope,
Have much to say about the fascination
1240   Of abstract rhetoric over us. Their research
Must certainly result in speculation
On the breakdown of idiom, the confusion
In style and personality, and the trend
Away from national language toward—what?
For one thing they will notice the intrusion
Of foreign forms and phraseology;
For another, the multitude of our translations;
And thirdly, the advent of those dialects
Peculiar to our age of rime. This section
1250   Will attempt to touch upon these three aspects
Of language and their reference to our art.

Before our time the explanatory use
Of Greek and Latin ribbons of quotation
Was limited to the heading of the poem;
The actual insertion of a tag
Of foreign meaning into one's own text
Is a more recent innovation, indeed
A characteristic of our outward form.

The *Cantos* have accustomed us to find
1260   The polyglot in the studio; our poets
Swear in the Sanskrit and the Portuguese.
We take the word of Eliot that *da-ta*
And *coco-rico* have their definitions,

And dare not smile when English is not enough.
We must have new glossarial editions
And variora on final variora,
Headnotes and footnotes and appendiceal JABBERWOCKY
Behindnotes to the poem. I do not scoff,
I merely ask; I merely quote MacLeish,
Signora, it is true the Greeks are dead 1270
And sadly add, but jabberwocky lives.

One might have glanced ahead in 1910
And seen the advent of the rime translation
As it is known to us; nor would he then
Have questioned the advantage and the value
Of this revival. Spanish and German rime,
The immediate interchange of foreign genius
Could work no injury upon the English
Or contravene the idiom—which it did
Nevertheless. It may be we can rival 1280
Murray, Cary and Lang in rendering
The foreign poem; I am not qualified
To say. Our present argument, however, THE
Pertains to the effect of rime translation IMITATION OF
Upon the English poem. In the contemporary TRANSLATION
Anthology one seems to read at times
A dialect of a dialect, translation
Where no original exists. I mean
The rime of conscious foreign overtones,
Not merely structures like asyndeton 1290
And un-English inversion and the like.
For so suggestible is the modern poem
That out of Spender's Rilke comes a style
The English of which is copied in our verse
As a new idiom. One cannot impugn
The motives of the translator in the least,
But as the fashion of the pony-text
Has increased and become a serious mode,

Our native rhetoric has taken on
1300   An international accent, not unlike
A learned pidgin or a code. Rimbaud,
Lorca and Baudelaire may be adduced
As three whom, in our heated admiration,
We have abused outrageously. And note
That neither Binyon, Eliot nor MacNeice
Has in his renderings of a foreign tongue
Impressed us in this manner. I believe
The reason lies in how more than in what
They translate. They maintain the character
1310   Of their own rime and do not simulate
The linguistic quality of the thing translated.
That English style has suffered through the adoption
Of forms somehow derived from alien speech
Cannot be overlooked, however; nor should
The damage done be underestimated.

Of those who have evolved a dialect,
An idiom or what you will from sources
Beyond the English boundary, the worst
Offenders are Americans. The forces
1320   Which drive us to these curious practices
I will attempt to point out in the following
Chapter. Meanwhile let us examine one
Exponent of this school, and that the chief,
A poet of bitter enemies and a man
Of vast influence in our literature.
MacLeish, contrary to professional
Opinion on this score, has shown a single
Development in his style throughout. His quest
For the total comprehensible in the word
1330   Has carried him, like Pound, around the world
And to and fro in time. What languages
Intermingle and fuse in both these poets
I cannot say, but it is my belief

That the Librarian indicates his way
In such poems as the one on Andrew Marvell
And that on Einstein. His intrinsic faith
In the destiny of his social man equates
With his obsession for the oracle,
The language of warning and the prophecy.
The motion of his mind is east to west,
The opposite to Pound's; nor does he rest
With the discovery of his native land,
But voyages beyond to the Just City,
The beloved optic illusion of our rime.
One moment at the caravansary
Is all; we hear *la longue haleine, the horn
Of Roland in the passages of Spain,*
The most triumphant and the saddest verse
This poet has rimed; and the conquistador
Is restlessly away—where and how far?
And now we hear the blood-curdling cry
The helmet is hollow! surely the most defeated
And baffled verse in all of modern rime.
Inevitably a special speech is born
Out of this searching, something absolute,
Something abstract beyond the endemic forms
Of English and the Romance. In this tongue
The inversions have no prototype; the particles
And the connectives in particular are endowed
With definite emphasis; and the participles
Flowing from line to line lead on the eye
Hypnotically; the prosody scarcely ripples.
The end-effect is a linguistic dream.
And one remembers Pound and Gertrude Stein,
Eliot and all the users of that prose
Which had its birth in Paris in the years
When Joyce sat in their midst. MacLeish is one
Who acted on the conspiracy of tongues
To found an influential dialect;

1340

1350

1360

1370 And Joyce provided the reductio
For the entire movement in one book,
His last, which moves beyond the linguistic line
Into the realm of Freudian philology.

It would be rash to say that we have failed
The King's and President's English in our art,
But it would be conservative to deny
That we are English-shy. Bad education,
The primacy of the journalese, the part
The pseudo-semantic sciences have played,
1380 The atomization of time-honored forms,
The nervousness of genius in our era,
The rapid pulse of the morphology
Of English in our day—these are but a few
Of the untoward conditions under which
Our rime has labored. Indeed, and we have paid
For poetry with living blood. What age
But ours can boast this terrifying truth?
Nor can we minister the antidote
To art, to science or to society
1390 Through more and more and more analysis.
We must not now embroider the confusion;
Toward language we must show the piety
Of simple craftsmen for their wood. I wish
I might agree with Yeats in his opinion
That in our forty years we have produced
More poets of worth than any generation
From 1630 on! Were we so good
These vices of our rime would not be loosed
So carelessly upon us. We would find
1400 More art, more love, more poetry of the kind
That Yeats bequeathed, and less verse of the mind.

THE CONFUSION
IN BELIEF

3

1. THE FAILURE IN BELIEF

I made a statement on the previous page
That we have paid for poetry with our blood,
A tabloid fact which sounds unfortunately
Misplaced in an essay. But I refer
To one who is the martyr of this age
Of rime, a man whose suicide confounds
The biographer and the critic. I mean Hart Crane,
The poet of our industrial success,
Whose death was equally an act of shame,   1410
Bewilderment and contrition. How else explain
The self-murder of this talent that stands higher
Than any, excepting our expatriates,
Since Whitman? Where in all his verses lies   POETRY
Concealed the clue to his destruction? What   AND SUICIDE
In this short life suggests the violent death?
One says his mystic nature, the hand of fire,
Another his maladjustment, and a third
Dissatisfaction with the century.
These are not answers. Add to any one   1420
Of the above a psychopathic complement
And one might have the formula; but Crane
Supplies us with no clinical evidence
To make the diagnosis neat. Of all
The famous suicides of modern art
From Nietzsche on, this baffles more than any,
Is the most terrible of all because
Committed in cold blood, apart from love,
Apart from hate, apart from sure belief.

Let us not reckon the statistics of   1430
Those artists who have left the pencilled note,
The unpaid debt to life, and with less grief
Than expectation fell; but only ask
What deadly distillate of the heart is this

That kills the man most dearly pledged to live?
And, think, is not this dram the same that draws
The artist into self-imposed exile,
And some to self-imagined hell, and some
To infamous hatred of the thing they write?

1440 Crane died for modern rime, a wasted death;
I make the accusation with the right
Of one who loved his book; died without cause,
HART CRANE Leaped from the deck-rail of his disbelief
To senseless strangulation. When we shall damn
The artist who interprets all sensation,
All activity, all experience, all
Belief through art, then this chief suicide
May be redeemed. How many blind survivors,
Though ignorant of the logic of Crane's end,
1450 Continue in his steps. Or can it be
That we need deep-sea divers to bring back
His book, his body, and his memory?

The history of the creative arts is long
But the belief in art as the supreme
Criterion of experience is as new
As the electric light. Our poets belong
In dangerous numbers to this strange persuasion.
Small wonder that they live like ghosts and perish
Without biographies; small wonder too
1460 That they adopt an adjective for their name
And soberly defer to those who wear
The title of Intellectual. Poets by hosts
THE INTEL- Spring fully armed from pure obscurity
LECTUALS To bay like demons at us and to slay
The man in front; our brawls are commonplaces.

No one with half a dozen poems in print
Can have failed to notice the competitive

52

And not unseldom ugly mood of rime
And criticism. We are not known for graces
In modern art. A young and tender poet 1470
Perhaps must necessarily be led
Barefooted over broken glass to make
His introduction, but once installed the threat
To person and reputation is not removed.
We mourn each other at each work and cry
Alas with emphasis; one can hear the sighs
Of deep relief at every new demise.
I exaggerate intentionally. I have known
A celebrated critic of refined
Intelligence to praise a book in terms 1480
Of personal envy! Pained by his own pleasure
The critic in his strange discomfiture
Feels his security attacked by any

And all achievements. Such is our position
That one finds random articles which prove
(In the tradition of logical suicide?)
That rime should not be written after all.
Nor can we take other than literally
The bland and terrible rationale of Mari-
Anne Moore, who, speaking of contemporary 1490
Art, has declared in rime *I too dislike it.*

The history of the failure in belief
Is an encyclopedic inquiry. One
Cannot pretend to know the evidence
Or correlate the theories of our fall
From faith, from reason, and from natural science.
Yet the most cursory of investigations
Into our narrow subject must address
The greater problem. All rime more or less
Has a religious ancestry, for man, 1500
The evidence says, is a believing being.
Nor does it follow that the civilized,

The secular and the profane in art must fail
For lack of faith—thus too the evidence.
What here pertains is the solicitude
Of modern artists for their missing gods,
Our attitude of nervous self-defence
Against the emotions roused by great belief,
Our purely literary use of Christ
1510 In painting, prose and rime, our use of Christ
In any cynical neo-Christian sense
Or even with that perfunctory good-will
Which characterizes Tolerance. Eliot alone
By naming faith a positive attribute
Has justified this interest in belief,
But for the rest we cannot well condone
The anxious protestations of the poor
In faith, conviction, bias or what you will.

By now the plaints of Arnold are too stale
1520 For repetition, yet it is curious
I think to make comparison of his lush

THE CON-
SCIOUSNESS
OF DISBELIEF

Nostalgia for the Age of Faith with ours
Which is nostalgia madly furious.
In part that deep Victorian melancholy
Is father to our more frantic abnegation
Of all the supernatural. Rime must refer
Anti-religiously to belief and nature,
Or else create the kind of nomenclature
Which hints at natural science. The word *mystic*
1530 Today denotes a psychological
Condition, or some freak of human reason.
It is at once a kind of compliment
And an apology. All our adulation
For Blake seems centered in his Prophecies,
Those books which are the modern prototype
Of original mysteries, and yet who reads
Or writes about the *Songs of Innocence*?

Their perfect poetry cannot move the mind,
And we who have no heart to walk with beauty
Remain in undecided speculation   1540
Among the personal mysteries of his art.

2. NEW AND SUBSTITUTE BELIEFS

Thus not the failure in belief disturbs
Our rime, but our concern, anxiety
And anguished desperation at this failure.
Nor can we stomach simple piety
Except as an outlandish manifestation
Of genius, as in Thompson, Eliot
Or Hopkins. Our morality is abstract
To an absurdity; ethics and human law
Suffice the artist and the common man   1550
Today. This is what D. H. Lawrence saw
And raged at with such understandable
Fury that in the end he learned to hate   AMORALISTS
The victims of amorality as much
As senseless amorality itself.

The age which Aldous Huxley satirized
Is not yet over; all of his grotesques,
Believers and misbelievers are still abroad,
The hermit biologist and the self-outlawed
Political extremist, and our new friend   1560
The artist-critic smothered in his notes
And such a slave to comment that no poem
Or novel ever actually takes shape
In its free form. This same phenomenon
We meet in poets who grovel for allusion,
The point of reference, and the authority,
Seeking by means of this substantiation

To exchange confusion for a substitute
Belief, a fragment or a total system.

1570   One wonders what the youth of Darwin's day
Felt at his dread conclusion that the mind
Of God-created man differs from that

    Of the Quadrumana only in degree
    And not in kind. I daresay he fell mute,
    Though possibly he merely yawned; the world
Had come that distance from the sphere of faith
Before the evolutionist; some despaired,
Some paid no heed, but the significant
In art caught the Spencerian contagion

1580   And prophesied the new and perfect man.
Nor can it be denied that man in spirit
Had suffered a traumatic shattering shock.
The organic chain of human breeding-stock
Saw the last mystery dispelled. The eye
Appraised the man as beast, the beast as man,
Sometimes with preference for the lower form.
There is a passage in *The Descent of Man*
Which matches in distemper Whitman's cry
I think I could turn and live with animals.

1590   Man as the reasoning beast thus elevated,
Freed from the mystic symbol of authority,
Superior to the past and sanguine of
Tomorrow, now like a revolutionist
Paraded his intentions and his pride
Of universal ownership. The hatred
Of man's condition found philosophy
At its disposal, and the Age of Reason
(With a slight German accent) walked beside
The Age of Progress toward the Age of War.

1600   I use these reckless terms advisedly
And in defiance of the semantic muse;

Who are the lineal ancestors of the Reds,
The Browns, the Blacks I do not think applies
In this context, nor does it here pertain
That Pound claims Jefferson for the Fascist side
And Auden Voltaire for the opposite.
The fact remains that from the synthesis
Of cries for progress and equality
A substitute belief had taken shape
And with it an esthetic corollary.   1610
The rape of deity had laid bare the brute
Heart of the economic absolute
The Christian content of which was false, a play
On words, a radical velleity.   THE MARXIST
No poem in modern English is more stark,   POET
More hideous and more brilliant than *The Funeral*,
Spender's omega of our disbelief.
Also I think it curious to remark
That Lenin, laughing at the new esthetic,
Declared that he preferred the art of Pushkin   1620
To that of Mayakovsky. What if the ear
Of that tall Soviet poet had overheard
His leader's passing comment? For the poet
Of Communism died by his own hand,
Implying what disaster and what fear?

Art insofar as it involved the faith
In revolution helped disprove itself
And its dependent theory. Before Spain
A brief light glowed, a hope for poetry
As it was thought, but in the great blackout   1630
And the ensuing night the poets dispersed
To take up arms or chew the bitter end
Of doubt, or ruminate their sad conclusion.
Two men escaped the heartache and the trial
Of readjustment in belief, MacNeice
And Barker, both of Auden's influence;

The first a man of more Horatian tastes
Than any modern that we know, the second
A man whose human-heartedness refused
1640   The exultant Marxist signal while it beckoned.

The Age of Science has sired no belief
More serviceable to the artist of lost faith
Than Freud's deterministic therapy.
Had this great German not himself exploited
The farthest implications of his findings,
His impress on the painting and the poem
Would not perhaps be felt in our own day.
The fact, however, is that the full genetic
Theory of human conduct must embrace
1650   Each act of psychic history, in the race
Or in the individual. Myth and fable,
A great national decision or a slip
Of the hostess' tongue, the dream, the accident,
The theft, the failure, and the sacrifice,
The repressive virtue and the compulsive vice,
All are fair game to the investigator.
And works of art, those creatures of the soul
Born of deep instinct and imagination,
These above all are keys to the dark psyche
1660   Which governs us. Surely there is no greater
Tribute to the creative mind than this,
At least in our own day. Art as a branch

THE FREUDIAN   Of clinical analysis has regained
POET   Some of its lost prestige as art. The end
Result none but a prophet can foretell;
Yet if the present evidence is arraigned
The work of Joyce alone would seem to stand
As positive proof of the expedient
Of rendering rime according to the laws
1670   Of the Unconscious—which is not the case.
Joyce did not use the junk-pile of the Id

To substitute for imagery and idea.
If anything *Ulysses* is a proof
And, in the sense of Schnitzler's works, a *cause*
Of psychoanalysis; nor can one imagine
Either the novelist or the great analyst
Approving the free-lance surrealist
In poetry, prose or paint. Rather I think
They must have held aloof from the makeshift
In style, imagination and belief.   1680

It is an unfortunate consequence of Freud's
Deductive therapy that the symbolism
Of laboratory and clinic have leaked out
Into the street. And yet the Viennese
Himself, and acting on the principle
Of the omniscience of his method, is
In the main responsible. For he hoped to train
The layman and not the doctor in his art,
And stressed mythology, history and religion
Rather than medicine. It is therefore   1690
No mystery to find among his works
An answer to the famous paradox
Of Hamlet's indecision. Using the case
Of Oedipus as a guide, the analyst
Tightens the noose around the prince's heart
And proves incestuous jealousy at the core
Of Hamlet's madness. The implication is,
And Freud makes it himself, that the playwright
Had known and suffered this profound psychosis.
Fortunately for us such arguments   1700
Lie well beyond the scope of this essay.
My point in bringing Hamlet to the fore
In this connection is to show the range
And territorial reach of this occult
Science. No man can make the accusation
That Freud was an empiricist in ideas;

It is the amateur who has vulgarized,
Distorted and abused his symbolism,
His nomenclature and his concepts. Poets
1710 Casting about for novelty and chic
Have fled to sexual imagery and dreams
As to a Moslem's paradise. I think
The apogee of this corrupt technique
Has found its place in Hollywood, the scene
Of many cultural horrors of our time.

3. PERSONAL SYSTEMS

By nineteen twenty the thin ice of belief
Had cracked and given way. The figure-skater
Of rime had sunk beneath the lake, and art
Took on a deep and submarine aspect.
1720 The corpse, the crawling rat, the bones, the wraith
Arrived in sequence; a whole world lay wrecked
And inundated. Prufrock filled with grief

POETRY And whimsical mockery walked along the beach,
OF DISBELIEF Envied the crab and heard the mermaid sing.
He toyed with death by drowning, fascinated
Like Arnold by the ebbing Sea of Faith.
Nor did the watcher understand his plight
In its true character, for *The Hollow Men,*
The Waste Land and *The Hippopotamus*
1730 All seemed the obituary of the spirit
For whose demise the worldly celebrants
Made this macabre music. What we know
In retrospect is that the prophet's eyes
Were turned toward the cathedral and the past
As toward a promise. But in the interim
Between his deep and masterly despair
And the overt fulfillment of his faith
His word was our poetic law. It is

Ironical that the monsters of his pen,
Sweeney and the young man carbuncular,   1740
Should have enhanced our widespread disbelief
In one another. The younger men who saw
A theological Anglican emerge
From the familiar cracked sarcophagus
Thought it a yogi or a New England witch.
A dirge for him was sounded from the left;
All thought it hollow to pursue the strange
Pied Piper of despair to church. Besides,
There were brave kids to follow to the grave
In Austria and Spain. The pain of death   1750
Was in that hour decorous and more sweet
Than life lived on the plane of accident,
Stagnation and the conspiracy of power.

So went a long procession to the war
In thirty-six, and left a leader home.   THE WAR POET
The choice of art for action was the last
Heroic stand of poetry in our time,
For in the final year of that decade
When the great war began, our poets were past
A reconciliation with the event,   1760
Dumb-struck to realize the tragic fall
Of their belief. Scarcely a one remained
Who could with conscience answer the first call
Of his own country. Those who went abroad
And those who slept in tunnels dropped the pen.
The rime produced by soldiers of our war
Is the most sterile of the century.

Here I would like to interject the point
That poetry insofar as it depends
Upon belief succeeds in ratio   1770
To the success of the belief itself.
If we consider this tautology

In the light of modern rime we can see why
So many poets lie dead upon the shelf.
I do not speak of truth; the artist may
Adjure the six heads of the Hindu lady,
The Blessed Virgin or the Greek Aphrodite,
But once the reader questions the integrity
Of the believer, the game is up; because
1780   Foremost we take for granted that the poem,
Though gravely false according to our lights,
Is given in good faith. Nor do we pause

To wonder if Shakespeare believed in sprites.
Yet in our day such is the anarchy
Of personal conviction and belief
That one cannot determine when the poem
Is fantasy, dream-symbolism, fact,
Or merely nonsense. Yeats, so we are told,
Invented a toy universe with gyres
1790   And spooky fires. We do not think that he
Believed in fairies and the pot of gold,
But what are we to say to his concern
With table-rapping and the great Blavatsky?
Rilke constructed a cosmography
For his own use in the Duino poems;
The chances are it was a Xanadu
And not a real belief, and yet who knows?
MacLeish once wrote a serious review
Of a great contribution to philosophy
1800   Which never existed. Why the practical joke,
The personal rearrangement of the stars,
The love, yet the contempt, for mysticism?
Dante believed in Hell, but the details
Which he legitimately conceived to fill
His page were the acknowledged images
Of art. Nor did the reader then confuse
The poet's belief with his imagination.
It is a condition of appreciation

That we accept the artist's premises
Wherever possible. When the Marxist muse   1810
Was queen, this was the simple thing to do,
But when the Marxist poet fell out with Marx
The system as a vehicle for its culture
Collapsed. In our own life-time we have seen
The biological cycle of an art
Complete itself and come to history.

Belief, it may be, is fortuitous
In rime; there are perhaps as many poets
Who shrug their shoulders at the word as there
Are those who clutch it like a talisman.   1820
Shakespeare, we think, believed in God and country
And the nobility of man. What else?
The greatest poet has left us no account
Of his theology or his metaphysics;
This in our day is almost tantamount
To calling him a fool or a barbarian.
Certain it is that we regard belief
As the tap-root of art. So various
And multifoliate are our breeds of faith
That we could furnish a herbarium   1830
With the American specimens alone.
A choice anthology of a few of these
Made its appearance just before the war;
It is an album of philosophies
Called *I Believe*. The essays it contains
Have nothing in common but proximity.

4. DIALECTIC AND CRITICISM

The bedlam of persuasions, personal creeds,
Opposing forms, methods of dialectics,
And their subjoined esthetics might be classed

1840   Together under the heading *Criticism*.
By criticism I do not mean the art
Of judging art, but the complex of mind
Which has beset the modern writer, that
Which is expressed through self-dependent pride
In thought, act and invention. Commonly
We call this Objectivity, though Locke
In a less positive age referred to it
As Prudence. Love of evidence and fact
Has narrowed vision and imagination
1850   In poetry to the vanishing-point. Our moral
Self-reliance in art disclaims the worth
And even the use of art. The frenzied poet
Exhausted in the half-lit cage of science,
Pretending faith and weak identity
With his subjective soul is not the Faust
Who stormed the door of Hell and roused the Devil.
Alas for us, the structural universe
Has neither good nor evil but only true
And false; we have the legend in reverse:
1860   Satan calls *us* to save him from ennui
And to display our knowledge of the earth.

The triumph of criticism is seen at last
In our alchemic search for what we call
The criterion and the value. Man as a spirit
Having been laid to rest by Sociology,
Psychoanalysis and Economics seeks
That to which substance can hold fast and yet
Be free as substance. In our neutrality
Of spirit we cannot countenance the soul
1870   Or treat with it except as ectoplasm,
That is with humor and sophistication.
Yet curiously we note a chronic spasm
Of guilt in rime suggesting that morality
As the conflict of inborn good and evil

In human nature is still a force. We play
Semantically upon these attributes
Which once were the omnipotent and perfect
Prongs of the magnet of all life and death,
And holding to this neutral course we claim
The discovery of a science in behavior,   1880
Our talk of which dilates on right and wrong,
Values in point-of-view, criteria
In taste, and criticism in everything.

One need but ask Where is the literature
Of nature, where the love poem and the plain
Statement of feeling? How and when and why
Did we conceive our horror for emotion,
Our fear of beauty? Whence the isolation
And proud withdrawal of the intellectual
Into the cool control-room of the brain?   1890
At what point in the history of art
Has such a cleavage between audience
And poet existed? When before has rime   THE POETRY
Relied so heavily on the interpreter,   OF IDEAS
The analyst and the critic? Finally how
Has poetry as the vision of the soul
Descended to the poetry of sensation,
And that translated to the perceptive kind,
Evolved into the poetry of ideas?
Perhaps it is that Poe was the last poet   1900
In the classic signification of the word;
Europe was quick to claim the furniture
Of his rich vision (and the sticks and props   THE POETRY
With which he stuffed his mansion) but the bird,   OF VISION
The princess, Helen herself, were dead.
Recumbent Poe before the deep backdrops
Became the Lenin of the Symbolists;
The yeast of criticism worked, and rime
Declined to verbiage, decomposed to forms.

65

The greatest of the logical suicides
During that century of fermenting art
Witnessed the great confusion and vowed silence;
This was Rimbaud, in whom the broken cry
To purify the word echoes the prayer
Of Baudelaire to purify the heart.

Nor is it any accident that Emerson
Anointed Whitman and not Poe. The nation
A hundred years ago was real estate
For the synthetic myth and poetry
1920 On the grand national-international scale.
I do not think that I exaggerate
In saying that our period has produced

THE POETRY More poems conceived as epics, large and small,
OF THE Than has the entire history of rime!
SYNTHETIC The bulk of these fall from the sanguine pens
MYTH Of Emersonian and Whitmanian bards;
These in their works, as if to justify
And prove our transcendental unity,
Recite the whole geography and construct
1930 A gigantic stage perennially set
For some Siegfried who never comes. How odd
That Sandburg turning from the likely god
Of this mythology deserts his rime
And turns to monumental scholarship
For his interpretation. The poet himself
Observes the overall imperative
Of criticism; poetry must wait on fact.
And we have seen that when the hero lifts
The vizor of his helmet to the gaze
1940 Of the ecstatic myth-mad populace
That it is nothing but a shell, a voice
Without a face, a brash and neutral horn
That amplifies our disappointed hopes
And sends them crashing broadcast in the city

With deafening demolition; air-raid, panic
And fall, on these discords this music ends.
Thus our instinct for heroism gropes
Like a blinded Samson in captivity
Only to pull the roof down on our heads
And by the inherent potency of belief
To wreck the temple, Dagon and ourselves.
Our unifying manic myth persists
To tempt the ambitious nevertheless and pledge
To art the quantum and the formula
Of a world-faith. Rime at the ragged edge
Of civilization weeps among the facts.

DEATH
OF THE HERO

1950

5. THE DEAD HAND AND EXHAUSTION
OF OUR RIME

With the instinctive vigilance of the great
Explorer, Freud in a final summary
Of psychoanalysis as a key to life
Denies its value as a Weltanschauung.
The founder of depth psychology disavowing
Philosophy and religion as the mummery
Of wishfulness and illusion turns at last
To total science as the remaining basis
For whole belief; nor does he minimize
The force and the persistence of past faiths
And present in the psychic scheme of things.
But of the arts—and here we end our tract
On rime—he briefly says that in the main
They are beneficent and harmless forms.
This is the sane perspective, one that brings
The beloved creative function back to scale.
We cannot end like Dante on the stars
Until we view them with the saintly gaze
Of humble men acknowledging our knowledge

1960

1970

ART AS
WELTAN-
SCHAUUNG

Of nothing. Though we pretend to walk on Mars
With its proposed canals, Platonic cities
And supermen, while in the grip of art
As Weltanschauung, we show that we have failed
1980 To cross the neutral void. Secure on earth,
The rime of pure belief, its spirit spent,
Tired, hysterical, diffuse and vain,
Beseeches such as Freud for sympathy
And is rejected. Ultimately, on pain
Of violent separation from the states
Of being, art in its disembodied forms
Wanders through life as through a mardigras
And maunders back upon the stroke of twelve
To black oblivion. Reconstructing night,
1990 The poet with painted and lack-lustre eye
Stares in the glass at pallid dawn and sees
The image of his sufficiency, a face
Wretched in weakness and a vibrant claw
Trailing a pen. From such ennui the poem
Takes its first line, digresses for a space,
Slips sidewise on a metaphor, proceeds
In doubt of its intention toward a pitch
Of mild mental excitement, strings its beads
Of meaning on the mended thread of rhythm,
2000 Comments its way to a conclusion which
Is nothing but the vestigial proof of nothing;
Or else in senseless violence on itself

THE TYPE
OF MODERN
POETRY Ends in a brawl of vocatives and a roar
Of "ancestral voices prophesying war."
This is the norm and type of modern rime
In the mid-century of our art; deny
The evidence if you will, but there are tiers
Of volumes marked and catalogued and sealed
At library temperature, and enough to lay
2010 A crowd of us forever in Potter's Field.
I do not mean to fix an epitaph

To this essay, or end on the dead note
Of disillusion. Lucky for all concerned
No man can kill the destined poem or breathe
A breath into the natural corpse of one.
To feel the stir of life, impounded sun
In rime is finally the pragmatic test;
Nor can we take the measure of the best
Except for our own time. In the long run
The crimes and fallacies of an age of art   2020
Are set beside its high deeds and its truths
In reasonable perspective. Not to stand pat
On this truism, however, or break the back
Of my own cause, I here should underline
The three confusions I have spoken of,
In Prosody, in Language, and in Belief.
That these aspects should terminate in grief
To art is our misfortune. In the above
I have tried to indicate no more than that
The aftermath of poetry should be love.   2030

This essay is intended in no sense
To be definitive. Nevertheless I hope
That for the man who shares these sentiments
It will express the argument against
The common style, and help solidify
The layman's confidence in a plainer art.
For the most part, the poets I have discussed
Are those who seem the best to illustrate
Our errors; covertly, I have employed
My own poems freely as examples. Thus   2040
What I have published elsewhere in the trend
Of modern rime, I criticize herein
Hopefully. For until our vices end
"I too transported by the Mode offend."

In the course of this inquiry I have tried
To keep my personal preferences aside;
Therefore there are no references to some
Of our most honored and most widely read
Poets. A certain few, particularly
Of the American Southern School and such   2050
Dissimilar names as Stevens, Aiken, Frost,
W. J. Turner, Barker and MacNeice
It was my purpose to discuss, but lacking
A whole opinion of their work I could not.
My dissertation will not seem complete
To all, even within its narrow scope.

The metric of this book is made upon
The classic English decasyllable
Adapted to the cadence of prose speech;
Ten units to the verse by count of eye   2060
Is the ground rhythm, over which is set
The rough flux and reflux of conversation.

I wish to make acknowledgment to Doctor
David Lovett of Baltimore, to whom
This volume, once a letter in verse form,
Was first addressed; to William Van O'Connor
For many helpful comments and the use
Of several of his studies; and to my wife
Who from a distance half the world around
2070 Has guided me in this experiment
With gentleness and intelligence, which I pray
I have rewarded in this verse essay.

Netherlands East Indies
November, 1944